Science in a flash

Living things

Georgia
Amson-Bradshaw

W
FRANKLIN WATTS
LONDON • SYDNEY

Franklin Watts
Published in Great Britain in paperback in 2018 by The Watts Publishing Group

Copyright © The Watts Publishing Group 2017

Produced for Franklin Watts by
White-Thomson Publishing Ltd
www.wtpub.co.uk

Credits
Series Editor: Izzi Howell
Series Designer: Rocket Design (East Anglia) Ltd
Series Consultant: Philip Parker

The publisher would like to thank the following for permission to reproduce their pictures:
Images from Shutterstock.com: Potapov Alexander 4l, JIANG HONGYAN 4bl, Eric Isselee 4r, Soyka 5br, Tuzemka 5t, Eric Isselee 5l, Coffeemill 5, ilikestudio 5b, Alena Brozova 5tl, Tsekhmister 5b, ActiveLines 8, Jez Bennett 11, Iryna Art 11, Spreadthesign 12r, Anna Shakirova 12br, WhiteDragon 13l, alinabel 13, Maquiladora 13br, Sergey Zaykov 13, Dionisvera 15r, Kazakova Maryia 15, Designua 14l, snapgalleria 17, openeyed 18,Glass and Nature 21tr, Jakinnboaz 21, Petr Tkachev 20, Kazakova Maryia 22, Marta Jonina 25, Bonnie Taylor Barry 24t, Kazakova Maryia 27t, VectorShow27t, Everett Historical 26l
Illustrations by Steve Evans: 4tr, 4br, 5r, 5b, 11bl, 11br, 17c, 18bl, 19c, 25t, 26br, 27
Images from wiki commons: Lilac Breasted Roller 10l, Rainer Altenkamp10r, Dr. Günter Bechly 23t

Every attempt has been made to clear copyright. Should there be any inadvertent omission
please apply to the publisher for rectification.

ISBN 978 1 4451 5277 6

Printed in China

Franklin Watts
An imprint of
Hachette Children's Group
Part of The Watts Publishing Group
Carmelite House
50 Victoria Embankment
London EC4Y 0DZ

An Hachette UK Company
www.hachette.co.uk

www.franklinwatts.co.uk

In this book you'll see some words shown in **bold**. These are described on the glossary page at the back of the book .

Contents

What IS a LIVING THING?

Living things all have seven life processes in common.

Have you heard of MRS GREN? The name is famous among scientists. Don't worry if you're feeling a bit baffled, MRS GREN is here to explain! Her name stands for the seven different life processes, or characteristics that every living thing has in common. The seven processes are ...

Check out my moves!

Movement

All living things move. Animals move to hunt for food or avoid predators, while plants move (slowly) towards the light.

Reproduction

All living things reproduce. Animals have babies, and most plants make seeds to continue the **species**.

Sensitivity

Living things are sensitive to their environment. For example, mussels close when the tide goes out. Plants can tell which direction light is coming from, and which way is down.

Did you know?

The scientific word for 'living thing' is 'organism'.

4

Growth

Living things grow. They start small and get bigger.

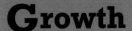

Respiration

Respiration is the name for the process where living things turn food into energy through chemical reactions in their **cells**.

I'm so full of ENERGY!

Excretion

When living things get rid of waste it is called 'excretion'. All living things do this.

Err, a bit of privacy, please?

Nutrition

All living things take in food or minerals in order to be able to respire and grow.

Om nom nom ...

POP QUIZ!

Which life processes are being described below?
Answer on page 28.

a) Chicken laying an egg
b) Butterfly drinking nectar
c) Crocus blooming in spring

Types of LIVING THING

We put living things into groups based on their similarities and differences.

Scientists think there are about 8.7 million different species of living thing on Earth. In order to help understand and study all the different organisms, scientists classify them, or put them into groups, based on the things they have in common.

Vertebrates
This group contains all animals with a backbone. It is a large group that is further divided into fish, birds, reptiles, **mammals** and **amphibians**.

Kingdom of funghi
This group includes mushrooms, yeasts and mould. They were once classified as plants, but they do not make their food through **photosynthesis**.

Kingdom of protists
Protists are organisms made of just a single cell. Some use whip-like threads to move around. They mostly live in water.

Five kingdoms
There are five main types of living thing, which are called the 'five kingdoms'. Within the five kingdoms there are further divisions.

Non-flowering plants

This group includes plants such as ferns and mosses, as well as coniferous trees such as pine and fir trees.

Flowering plants

Plants with flowers evolved later than the early, non-flowering types. Read about the life-cycle of a flowering plant on pages 16 and 17.

Invertebrates

These are animals that don't have a backbone. It includes creatures such as worms and jellyfish, as well as animals with a hard **exoskeleton** such as crabs or insects.

Kingdom of monera

Monera are the simplest living things. They were the first type of life to exist on Earth. **Bacteria** are in this kingdom.

Kingdom of plants

Plants are split into flowering and non-flowering types.

Kingdom of animals

Animals are split into **vertebrates** and **invertebrates**.

Now then, what am I?

WHAT IS A HABITAT?

A habitat is the type of place where a living thing lives.

Broadleaf woodlands, mountain grasslands, freshwater lakes, coral reefs – these are all types of **habitat**. Each type of habitat has a unique landscape, climate and selection of plants and animals living there.

No place like home

Each living thing has a particular habitat, or type of place that it can live. Different animals need different things, which is why they live in different habitats. For example, a fish needs water to swim in. A cold-blooded snake needs warmth from the Sun to move around. A zebra needs grass to graze on.

FACT ATTACK

Adaptation

The ways an animal is suited to its habitat are called **adaptations** – read about this on pages 10 and 11.

Gotta catch some rays.

Habitats under threat

There are lots of different types of habitat on Earth, but many of them are under threat from **climate change** and other human activity, such as **deforestation**.

Go pond dipping to explore a watery habitat.

You'll need a fine net, a light-coloured shallow tray, and some animal identification books or sheets from the Internet.

Fill your tray with pond water. Quietly look into the pond for a minute or two, to see what is moving around. Then, slowly lower your net into the water and move it gently a few times in a figure-of-eight motion.

Lift it out, and empty it into the water in your tray. What creatures have you caught? Can you identify them? Don't forget to put them back!

ALWAYS TAKE CARE AROUND DEEP WATER!

Nice neighbours?

Many plants and animals will share a habitat. Different species are able to live together in the same place because they fit into the **ecosystem**. This means they all have different jobs which keep the habitat healthy and in balance.

My job in the habitat is spreading pollen between flowers, helping more plants to grow.

What are ADAPTATIONS?

Animals develop different behaviours and appearances to stay alive.

Adaptations are a plant or animal's characteristics; things such as what it looks like, whether it lives in groups or alone, whether it is active during the day or night, and special ways its body works.

Day 43, they still think I'm a tree stump.

Potoo birds hunt at night. During the day they 'hide' on tree stumps.

Now you see me ...

One type of adaptation is **camouflage**. Animals use camouflage to blend in with their surroundings and hide. Predators can use camouflage to sneak up on their prey. Prey use camouflage to try and protect themselves from the predators' beady eyes!

Riddle me this!

There is a spider hiding in this picture. Can you find it?

Answer on page 28!

The best behaviour

Working together in groups, or packs, is a behaviour adaptation. Animals, such as wolves and lions, work together in teams, making them more powerful or safer than when they are alone. By working together lions can bring down large prey.

Migration is another behaviour adaption where animals, like these wildebeest below, move around to find food or breeding grounds.

Did you know?

The way that different species develop adaptations over time is called **evolution**. Read about this on pages 26 and 27.

Design an effective camouflage pattern for your 'habitat'. You'll need a piece of paper, scissors and colouring pencils.

Cut a butterfly shape out of paper. Imagine that your home is a wild habitat. Look around you at the shapes and colours you can see.

Colour a pattern onto your paper butterfly so that it will be camouflaged somewhere in your home.

Place your coloured butterfly where you think it will be best disguised, but don't hide it behind other objects!

Challenge a friend to see if they can see your butterfly that is hidden in plain sight.

Here the butterfly is 'hiding' on a cushion!

WHAT ARE FOOD CHAINS?

Living things are linked together by what they eat.

An ecosystem is a habitat, and the community of plants and animals that live there. In each ecosystem, the living things interact with each other, and they are all linked by their feeding habits. Plants become food for animals, who in turn become food for other animals: this process is called a **food chain**.

A food chain

1 Grass makes food from the Sun.

2 A grasshopper eats the grass.

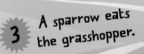
3 A sparrow eats the grasshopper.

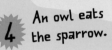
4 An owl eats the sparrow.

Producers and consumers

Within a food chain, the plants are called **producers**, because they use the Sun's energy to produce food. Animals do not produce food directly from the Sun, so they are called **consumers**.

A panda is a consumer.

Bamboo is a producer.

Eat or be eaten

Animals can also be divided up into **predators** and **prey**. A predator is an animal that eats another animal. Prey are the animals that get eaten. Ecosystems have a mix of producers, predators and prey.

A gerbil is a prey animal.

A cat is a predator.

Be afraid ... be very afraid ...

1 Phytoplankton make food from the Sun.

The seafood menu

Producers, consumers, predators and prey are found in the oceans and in rivers, too. The main producers in the oceans are **phytoplankton**, which are microscopic plants that float in the water. They are eaten by **zooplankton**, which are teeny tiny ocean animals.

2 Zooplankton eat phytoplankton.

3 A mackerel eats zooplankton.

FACT ATTACK
Plankton

Plankton are very important to our climate! Phytoplankton make around 70 per cent of the oxygen in the air through photosynthesis.

4 A shark eats the mackerel.

ALL ABOUT PLANTS

Plants are living things that take energy directly from the Sun.

From a tiny daisy to a giant oak tree, plants come in many shapes and sizes. Some of them are downright weird, like the rafflesia, which has the world's biggest flower. It gets to a metre across and smells like rotting meat – yuck! But plants are absolutely essential to the rest of life on Earth.

Light lunch

Plants form the basis of all life on Earth, because they take in the energy from the Sun to create food that other creatures can eat. They do this through a process called photosynthesis.

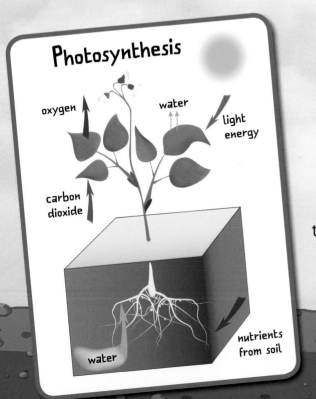

Photosynthesis

oxygen

water

light energy

carbon dioxide

water

nutrients from soil

Sun catchers

Plants capture sunlight through their leaves. They take in carbon dioxide gas from the air and water from the ground through their roots. Using energy from the Sun they change these into oxygen and sugar.

Fabulous flowers

The flower is the reproductive part of a plant, where new seeds are made. Flower petals are often brightly coloured and scented to attract insects. Inside the flower are the female parts which are called the 'carpel', and the male parts called the 'stamen' which carry pollen.

Something smells good!

Riddle me this!

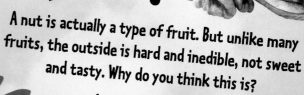

A nut is actually a type of fruit. But unlike many fruits, the outside is hard and inedible, not sweet and tasty. Why do you think this is?

Answer on page 28!

Juicy fruit

The job of the fruit is to protect developing seeds, and to then move them away from the plant. Many types of fruit are sweet and tasty to encourage animals to eat them, then drop the seeds in their poo.

Strong roots

Plants needs roots to suck up water and nutrients from the soil, as well as to anchor the plant safely in the ground.

Now, where are my strawberries?

The LIFE CYCLE of a PLANT

Most plants grow from a seed and reproduce through pollination.

Plant life cycles are a bit different depending on whether or not they are a flowering or a non-flowering species. The majority of plants on Earth are flowering plants, and their life cycle follows this basic pattern:

3

It grows a bud, which opens into a flower; the plant's reproductive part. Inside the flower is pollen.

2

The stem and leaves poke out above the soil. The plant grows bigger, taking in nutrients from the soil and energy from the Sun.

1

In the soil, a seed starts to sprout. It grows roots downwards, and a stem sprouts upwards.

See the first stages of a plant's life cycle by sprouting seeds in a plastic bag.

You'll need cress seeds, a paper towel, a stapler, a plastic zip-lock sandwich bag and tape.

Fold the paper towel so that it lays flat and fits inside the bag. Staple a row of staples horizontally through the plastic bag and paper towel. This makes a mini-pocket where the seeds can sit.

Pour some water into the bag so that it mostly soaks into the towel with a little extra water at the bottom. Next, place the seeds inside so they are sitting on top of the line of staples.

Seal up the bag and tape it to a window. Watch over a few days as the seeds begin to grow.

4

Pollen gets carried to a different flower by insects or by the wind. This is called **pollination**. At the second flower, the pollen joins the egg cells in the **ovary**, creating seeds.

5

Seeds often grow inside a fleshy coating, called a fruit. Animals and birds will eat the fruit containing the seeds.

6

The seeds are then scattered by animals or by the wind. This is called **dispersal**. The new seeds sprout in the ground and the cycle starts again.

ALL ABOUT MAMMALS

Mammals are warm-blooded animals that feed their young with milk.

If someone says 'think of an animal', you probably think of a mammal. Compared to other types of animal, they have big, intelligent brains. Humans are mammals too – the most intelligent mammal of all.

Amazing mammals

Mammals include farm animals , such as cows and pigs; pets, such as cats and dogs; and people's favourite wild animals, such as elephants and tigers. Mammals are found all over the world, from polar bears in the Arctic, to camels in the desert, and whales in the ocean.

Hey you! Mammal! Yes, I'm talking to you!

It's a mammal's life...

Most mammals have a similar life cycle, as shown in 1–4 here.

EYE SPY!

How many mammals can you see? Answer on page 29.

1 A pregnant adult female gives birth to live young, such as a lion giving birth to lion cubs.

2 Young mammals are small and cannot take care of themselves, so they are nursed (fed milk) by the parent and taught how to fend for themselves.

3 The next stage is adolescence, when the reproductive organs mature. In humans we call this stage 'puberty'.

4 After puberty, the mammal is a fully mature adult, ready to mate and have young of their own. Through mating, the adult female becomes pregnant, and the cycle begins again.

Baby you're purrrrfect ...

ALL ABOUT BIRDS

Birds are warm-blooded, feathered animals that lay eggs.

Squawk! Tweet! Chirrup! From a tiny hummingbird to a huge ostrich, birds come in all shapes and sizes. In fact, there are around 10,000 species of bird in the world, living in many different habitats.

Modern day dinosaurs

Fossils show us that birds evolved from small dinosaurs called theropods. This archaeopteryx fossil shows an animal that had wings and feathers like a modern bird, but still had toothed jaws, fingers with claws and a bony tail.

I'm an early bird. Literally.

Hollow bones

Birds have skeletons that are very strong, but hollow. This makes them much lighter, so they can fly. However, although most birds fly, not all do. Penguins are excellent swimmers, and ostriches can run faster than horses!

Help, I'm drowning!

No, you're swimming!

Life cycle of a bird

Bird behaviour can vary a lot. Some birds, such as weaver birds, build incredible nests, while others, such as guillemots, don't build a nest at all. But most birds have a similar life cycle, as shown in 1–4 here.

Weaver birds build long hanging nests.

4 As the chicks grow up, they get their adult feathers and learn how to gather their own food. Adult birds mate, and the female lays eggs in a nest to start the life cycle again.

1 Birds begin life inside a hard-shelled egg. The parent birds will keep the eggs warm by sitting on them, this is called **incubation**.

2 After a few weeks, the baby bird hatches out of the egg. At this stage it is called a chick.

3 Some chicks are born with downy feathers, and are able to move around. Other chicks are born completely featherless and blind, and depend on their parents to feed them.

All about AMPHIBIANS

Amphibians are animals that live both in water and on land.

The word amphibian comes from the Greek meaning 'two lives'. This is because they live their lives both on land and in water. Amphibians are cold-blooded, have thin, moist skin and lay eggs.

Shape shifters

Frogs and toads are amphibians. They begin life looking very different from their parents, and change shape in order to reach their adult form. This is called **metamorphosis**.

The amphibian life cycle has several stages, as seen in 1–4 here.

1 Most amphibians, including frogs, lay jelly-like eggs in water. These eggs then hatch into young.

2 The young of a frog or a toad is called a tadpole. Tadpoles live in water and breathe using gills, like fish do.

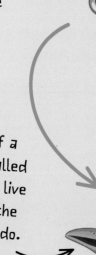

Ancient animals

The very first living things lived in water. Some ancient fish evolved into the first amphibians, such as ichthyostega, which lived partially in water and partially on land. Then, some of those amphibians evolved into reptiles, the first four-legged land animals.

ichthyostega

POP QUIZ!
Which of these creatures do you think is NOT an amphibian?
Answer on page 29.

a) salamandar

b) newt

c) gecko

Hey there princess, will you let me be your frog prince?

4 The froglets grow bigger and lose their tails completely, becoming adult frogs. Once the adult frogs are fully grown, they are ready to mate and lay eggs.

3 As the tadpoles grow bigger, they develop legs, and their tails shrink. Their gills are replaced by lungs, and they move out of the water onto land. At this stage they are called froglets.

All about INSECTS

Insects are invertebrates with six legs.

Unlike mammals, birds and amphibians, insects are invertebrates. This means they don't have a backbone. An insect is a particular type of invertebrate that has an exoskeleton, and six legs.

Billions of bugs

Insects are the most diverse type of animal on Earth. There are also loads of them – scientists estimate that there are more than 200 million insects for each human being on the planet! Insects range from tiny ants to bird-sized atlas moths.

Atlas moths can have a wingspan of 25 cm!

The insect life cycle

Like amphibians, most insects undergo metamorphosis.

2 The eggs hatch into caterpillars, which grow bigger by eating leaves of plants.

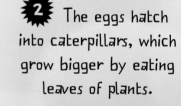

1 Adult butterflies and moths meet and mate, and then lay eggs on the underside of a leaf.

Give it a go!

Set up a moth trap to conduct a scientific survey of which moth species live in your local area. You'll need a clothes line and pegs, a bright light such as a powerful torch, a large white sheet and a camera with a flash to record your moths.

In your garden or another outdoor space, fix the clothesline between two trees or posts, and hang the sheet making a large white surface.

Hang your torch over the centre of the sheet so the sheet is brightly lit.

Wait until dark to see what moths come to your light. Record each species by taking a picture.

You could repeat your experiment at a different time of year or in a different location and compare the results.

3 When it gets big enough, the caterpillar forms a hard case around its body called a pupa.

EYE SPY!

Can you see any creepy-crawlies on this page that are NOT insects?

4 Inside the pupa the caterpillar's body breaks down and reforms. It then hatches out of the pupa in the form of a new butterfly or moth, ready to mate and reproduce.

25

What is EVOLUTION?

Evolution is the way living things change slowly over time.

Scientists believe life on Earth started with very simple single-celled organisms. Evolution is what has caused life on Earth to develop from those very first organisms into around 8.7 million different species that exist today.

The father of evolution

Charles Darwin developed the theory of evolution, which he published in his book 'Origin of Species' in 1859. His ideas are explained in 1–4 here:

Eeek!

Did you know?

There used to be other human species on Earth. Eventually they died out leaving only us, Homo Sapiens.

1 Some individual animals or plants in a species survive better than other individuals because they are better adapted – perhaps their camouflage is a bit better, or they are a bit bigger and stronger.

2 The individuals that survive go on to have more children, and so they pass on these characteristics to their offspring. This is called natural selection, and it explains how adaptations become common among species.

The green frog has more young.

3 The development of adaptations also explains how new species are created. For example, a single species of bird with a thin beak might spread out into different habitats, such as forests and grasslands.

thin-beaked bird

thick-beaked bird

thin-beaked bird

4 The birds that live in the forest might start to develop strong beaks which are better for cracking tree nuts. The birds that live on the grassland might eat insects and keep their thin beaks. Eventually the two groups become so different from one another that they become different species.

And the answer is ...

Page 5

Pop quiz:

a) shows reproduction. A chicken lays an egg which hatches into a new, baby chicken.

b) shows nutrition. A butterfly drinks sweet, sugary nectar to gain energy.

c) shows sensitivity. Crocus flowers are sensitive to when the temperature rises, letting them know that spring has arrived and it's time to bloom.

Page 10

Riddle me this:

The spider is camouflaged to look like just another bump on the twig!

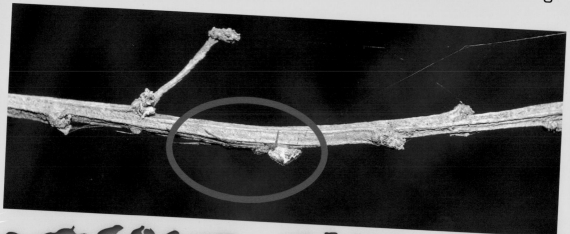

Page 15

Riddle me this: Plants use lots of different techniques to spread their seeds. Many package their seeds in sweet, tasty fruit to encourage animals to eat them and drop the seeds in their poo, or discard the seeds in a piece of the fruit that is not eaten. But some plants take the opposite approach. They cover their seeds with hard shells to protect them. Only animals with very strong teeth, such as squirrels, can open them. Hard shells keep the seeds safe until they drop to the ground and can sprout as new trees.

Page 19

Eye Spy: there are 46 mammals on pages 18 and 19, including the baby kangaroo and unborn lion cubs.

Page 23

Pop quiz: The answer is c) a gecko is not an amphibian, it is a reptile. It has dry, scaly skin, and lays its eggs on land.

Page 25

Eye Spy: the spider and the scorpion are NOT insects, they are arachnids.

Glossary

Adaptation A way that a living thing is suited to its environment

Amphibian A type of animal that lives in water and on land and undergoes metamorphosis

Bacteria Microscopic living things that have only a single cell

Camouflage Colours and patterns that help an animal blend in with its surrooundings

Cells Tiny building blocks that all living things are made of

Climate change Changes in the weather around the world due to global warming

Consumer A living thing that feeds on plants or other animals

Deforestation Destruction of forests by human beings

Dispersal When seeds are moved from the parent plant to a new growing site

Ecosystem A community of plants and animals in a habitat

Evolution How species change and develop over time

Excretion When a living thing gets rid of waste from its body

Exoskeleton Hard covering that supports and protects the bodies of some animals, such as crabs or beetles

Food chain How animals and plants are linked together by their eating habits

Habitat The place that plants and animals live

Incubation When a bird sits on its eggs to keep them warm

Invertebrates Animals without a backbone

Mammal A warm-blooded, hairy animal that is fed milk by its mother

Metamorphosis A change in an animal's appearance during its life cycle

Migration When animals travel to find food or safe places to breed

Nutrition When a living thing takes in food for energy and growth

Ovary The part of a plant where new seeds grow after pollination

Photosynthsis The process by which plants produce their own food using energy from the Sun

Phytoplankton Tiny microscopic ocean plants at the bottom of the ocean food chain

Pollination When pollen is transferred from one flower to another

Predator An animal that eats another animal

Prey An animal that gets eaten by another animal

Producer Green plants that make food through photosynthesis

Pupa The life stage of an insect where it creates a hard shell around its body

Reproduction When living things produce young of its species

Respiration A chemical process where living things turn food into energy

Sensitivity When living things react to changes in their environment

Species A group of living things that look alike and can breed with each other

Vertebrates Animals with a backbone

Zooplankton Tiny microscopic ocean animals

Further reading

Straight Forward with Science: Classification and Evolution
Peter Riley (Franklin Watts, 2015)

Disgusting and Dreadful Science: Slimy Spawn and Other Gruesome Life Cycles
Barbara Taylor (Franklin Watts, 2014)

Moving Up With Science: Plants   Peter Riley (Franklin Watts, 2016)

Secrets of Science: Habitats   Andrew Solway (Franklin Watts, 2014)

Websites

www.nhm.ac.uk/discover.html
Learn about living things through the Natural History Museum's collections.

pbskids.org/wildkratts/habitats/   Play online games and explore habitats.

www.bbc.co.uk/education/topics/z6wwxnb   Watch videos about living things.

Index

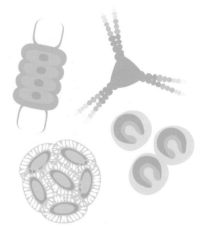